Contents

About Science Centers
Grades 1–2

What's Great About This Book

Centers are a wonderful, fun way for students to practice important skills. The 14 centers in this book are self-contained and portable. Students may work at a desk, table, or even on the floor. Once you've made the centers, they're ready to use any time.

What's in This Book

Teacher direction page includes how to make the center and a description of the student task

Full-color materials needed for the center

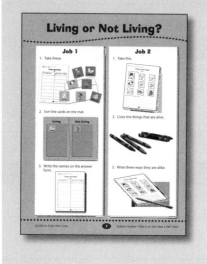

Reproducible answer forms

How to Use the Centers

The centers are intended for skill practice, not to introduce skills. It is important to model the use of each center before students do the task independently.

Questions to Consider:

- Will students select a center, or will you assign the centers?
- Will there be a specific block of time for centers, or will the centers be used throughout the day?
- Where will you place the centers for easy access by students?
- What procedure will students use when they need help with the center tasks?
- Where will students store completed work?
- How will you track the tasks and centers completed by each student?

Making a File Folder Center

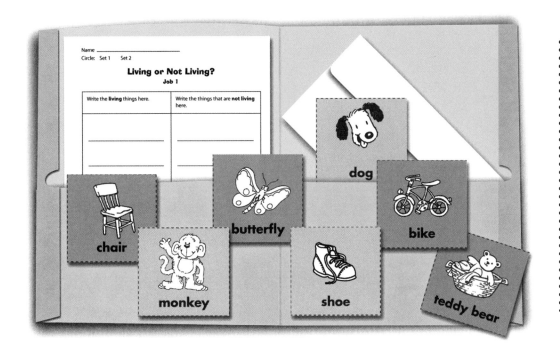

Folder centers are easily stored in a box or file crate. Students take a folder to their desks to complete the task.

Materials

- folder with pockets
- envelopes
- marking pens
- glue
- tape

Steps to Follow

1. Laminate the cover design. Glue it to the front of the folder.

2. Laminate the student direction page. Glue it to the back of the folder.

3. Place answer forms, writing paper, and any other supplies in the left-hand pocket.

4. Place each set of task cards in an envelope. Place the envelope and sorting mat (if required for the center) in the right-hand pocket.

Living or Not Living?

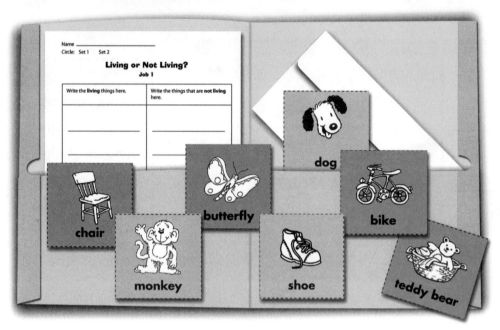

Prepare a folder following the directions on page 3. Laminate the cover design on page 5 and the student directions on page 7. Attach the cover to the front of the folder and the student directions to the back of the folder.

Preparing the Center

Job 1

1. Laminate the sorting mat on page 9 and the cards on pages 13 and 15. Cut the cards apart and place each set of cards in an envelope. Label the envelopes *Set 1* and *Set 2*.
2. Place the envelopes and the sorting mat in the right-hand pocket of the folder.
3. Reproduce the answer form on page 11 and place copies in the left-hand pocket of the folder.

Job 2

1. Reproduce the answer form on page 12.
2. Place copies in the left-hand pocket of the folder.

Using the Center

Job 1

1. The student chooses one set of cards and circles the set number on the answer form.
2. The student sorts the cards into two sets on the mat—living or not living.
3. Then the student writes the name of each item in the correct column on the answer form.

Job 2

1. Using page 12, the student colors the things that are alive.
2. Then the student lists three ways living things are alike.

Living or Not Living?

Living things eat.

A turtle eats. A rock does not.

Living things grow.

A turtle grows. A rock does not.

Living things move.

A turtle moves. A rock does not.

Living things reproduce.

A turtle reproduces. A rock does not.

Living or Not Living?

Job 1

1. Take these.

2. Sort the cards on the mat.

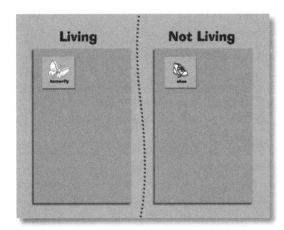

3. Write the names on the answer form.

Job 2

1. Take this.

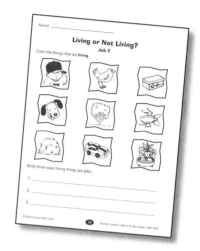

2. Color the things that are alive.

3. Write three ways they are alike.

Science Centers—Take It to Your Seat • EMC 5002

Not Living

Living

Name _____

Circle: Set 1   Set 2

Living or Not Living?

Job 1

Write the **living** things here.	Write the things that are **not living** here.
_____	_____
_____	_____
_____	_____
_____	_____
_____	_____

Name _____

Living or Not Living?

Job 2

Color the things that are **living**.

Write three ways living things are alike.

1. _____

2. _____

3. _____

turtle

rock

tree

shoe

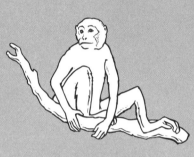

monkey

book

bird

box

dog

car

flower

flag

Set 1

Set 1

Set 1

Set 1

Set 1

Set 1

Set 1

Set 1

Set 1

Set 1

Set 1

Set 1

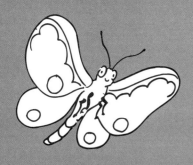

butterfly

fish

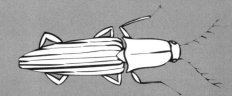

beetle

girl

duck

pony

chair

basket

bike

cookie

computer

teddy bear

Set 2

Set 2

Set 2

Set 2

Set 2

Set 2

Set 2

Set 2

Set 2

Set 2

Set 2

Set 2

What Goes Together?

Prepare a folder following the directions on page 3. Laminate the cover design on page 19 and the student directions on page 21. Attach the cover to the front of the folder and the student directions to the back of the folder.

Preparing the Center

Job 1

1. Laminate and cut out the cards on pages 25–29. Place the cards in an envelope. Label the envelope *What Goes Together?*
2. Place the envelope of cards in the right-hand pocket of the folder.
3. Reproduce the answer form on page 18 and place copies in the left-hand pocket of the folder.

Job 2

1. Reproduce the answer form on page 23 and the pictures on page 24.
2. Place copies in the left-hand pocket of the folder.

Using the Center

Job 1

1. The student looks at the cards and selects four items that go together in some way. He or she lists the four items on the answer form and explains how they are alike.
2. The student repeats the steps with four new cards.

Job 2

1. The student takes a copy of the answer form (page 23) and cuts out the pictures on page 24.
2. The student selects three pictures that are alike in some way, glues them in the boxes after number 1, and then writes about how they are alike.
3. Then the student selects three more pictures and repeats the process.

Name _____

What Goes Together?
Job 1

List 4 things that go together.

1. _____   3. _____

2. _____   4. _____

How are they alike?

_____

_____

_____

I have fur.

List 4 more things that go together.

1. _____   3. _____

2. _____   4. _____

How are they alike?

It flies.

_____

_____

_____

     Science Centers—Take It to Your Seat • EMC 5002

What Goes Together?

We go together. We all have wings.

Science Centers—Take It to Your Seat • EMC 5002

What Goes Together?

Job 1

1. Take these.

2. Pick four that go together.

3. Write the names.
   Write how they are alike.

4. Do it again with four more cards.

Job 2

1. Take these.
   Cut out the pictures.

2. Pick three that are alike.
   Glue them in the boxes on top.

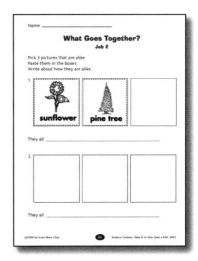

3. Tell how they are alike.

4. Pick three more things that are alike. Glue them in the boxes. Tell how they are alike.

Name _____

What Goes Together?
Job 2

Pick 3 pictures that are alike.
Glue them in the boxes.
Write about how they are alike.

1.

They all _____.

2.

They all _____.

Pictures for Job 2

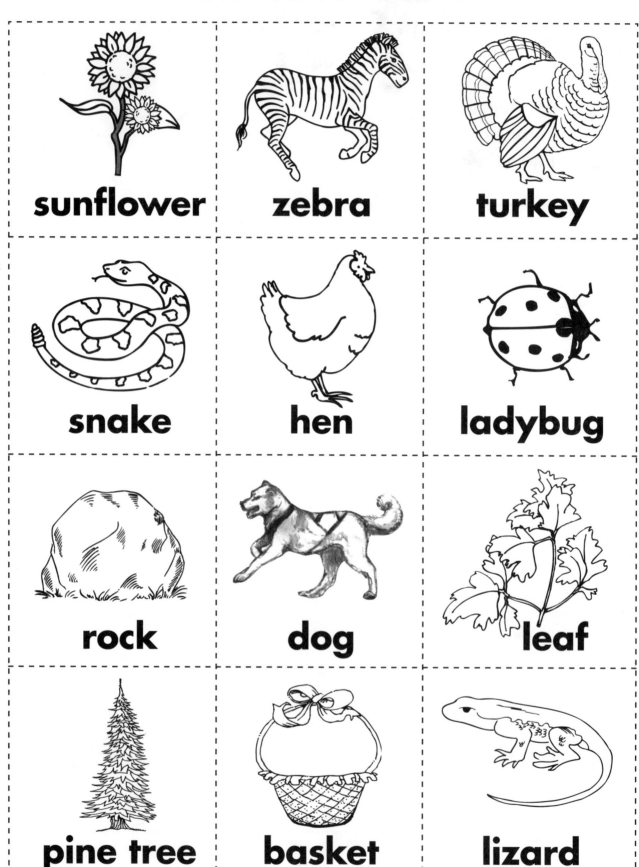

sunflower

zebra

turkey

snake

hen

ladybug

rock

dog

leaf

pine tree

basket

lizard

flowering plant

tree

bush

cactus

hawk

flamingo

parrot

penguin

bat

zebra

skunk

raccoon

squirrel

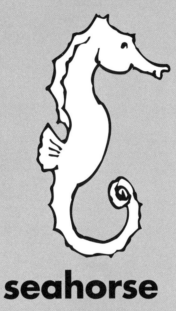

seahorse

shark

octopus

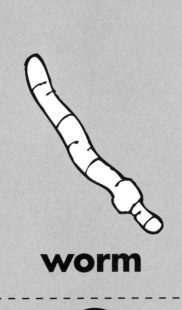

worm

salamander

frog

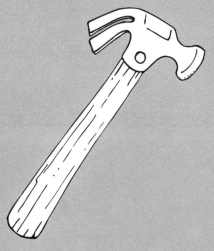

hammer

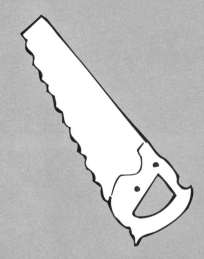

saw

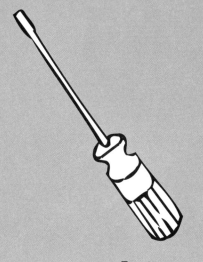

screwdriver

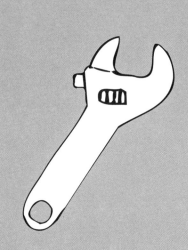

wrench

wagon

bicycle

car

motorcycle

Spiders and Insects

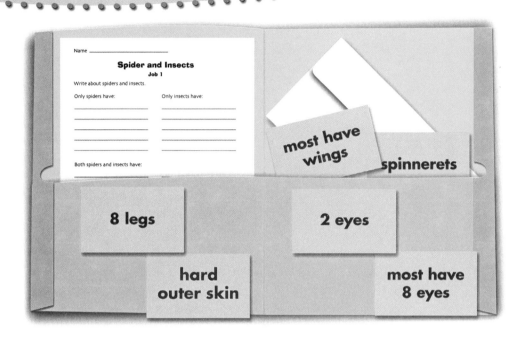
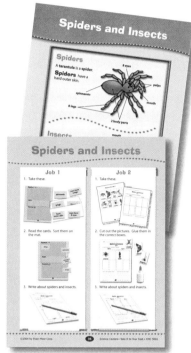

Prepare a folder following the directions on page 3. Laminate the cover design on page 33 and the student directions on page 35. Attach the cover to the front of the folder and the student directions to the back of the folder.

Preparing the Center

Job 1

1. Laminate the sorting mat on page 37 and the cards on page 39. Cut the cards apart and place them in an envelope. Label the envelope *Spiders and Insects*.
2. Place the envelope of cards and the sorting mat in the right-hand pocket of the folder.
3. Reproduce the answer form on page 32 and place copies in the left-hand pocket of the folder.

Job 2

1. Reproduce the answer form on page 41 and the pictures on page 42.
2. Place copies in the left-hand pocket of the folder.

Using the Center

Job 1

1. The student reads the cards and sorts them on the Venn diagram sorting mat.
2. Then the student lists what is true about each category on the answer form.

Job 2

1. Using pages 41 and 42, the student cuts out the pictures and glues them in the correct boxes.
2. Then the student writes an explanation describing how to tell which animals are spiders and which are insects.

Name _____

Spiders and Insects
Job 1

Write about spiders and insects.

Only spiders have:

_____

_____

_____

_____

Only insects have:

_____

_____

_____

_____

Both spiders and insects have:

_____   _____

Draw.

a spider	**an insect**

Science Centers—Take It to Your Seat • EMC 5002

Spiders and Insects

Spiders

A **tarantula** is a **spider**.

Spiders have a hard outside skin.

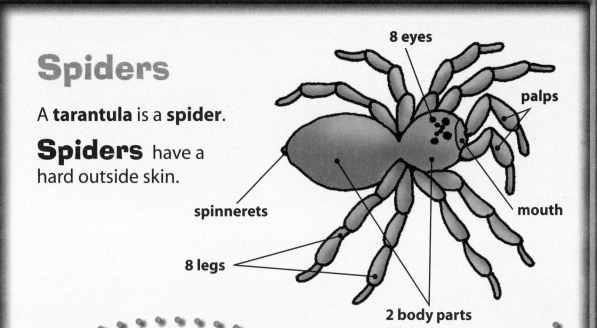

8 eyes

palps

mouth

spinnerets

8 legs

2 body parts

Insects

A **bee** is an **insect**.

Insects have a hard outside cover.

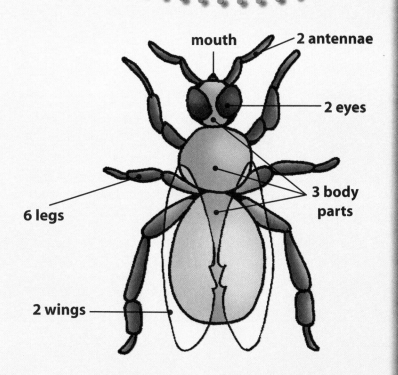

mouth

2 antennae

2 eyes

3 body parts

6 legs

2 wings

Science Centers—Take It to Your Seat • EMC 5002

Spiders and Insects

Job 1

1. Take these.

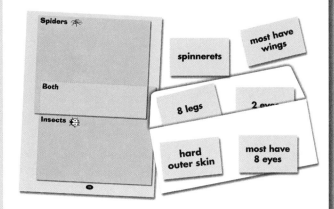

2. Read the cards. Sort them on the mat.

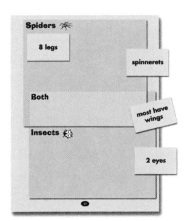

3. Write about spiders and insects.

Job 2

1. Take these.

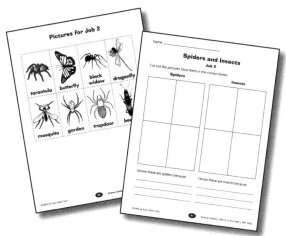

2. Cut out the pictures. Glue them in the correct boxes.

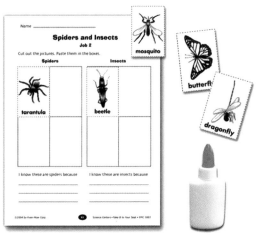

3 Write about spiders and insects.

Spiders

Both

Insects

8 legs	2 body parts	most have 8 eyes
spinnerets	palps	mouth
hard outer skin	6 legs	3 body parts
2 eyes	antennae	most have wings

Name _____

Spiders and Insects
Job 2

Cut out the pictures. Glue them in the correct boxes.

Spiders   **Insects**

I know these are spiders because   I know these are insects because

_____   _____

_____   _____

_____   _____

Pictures for Job 2

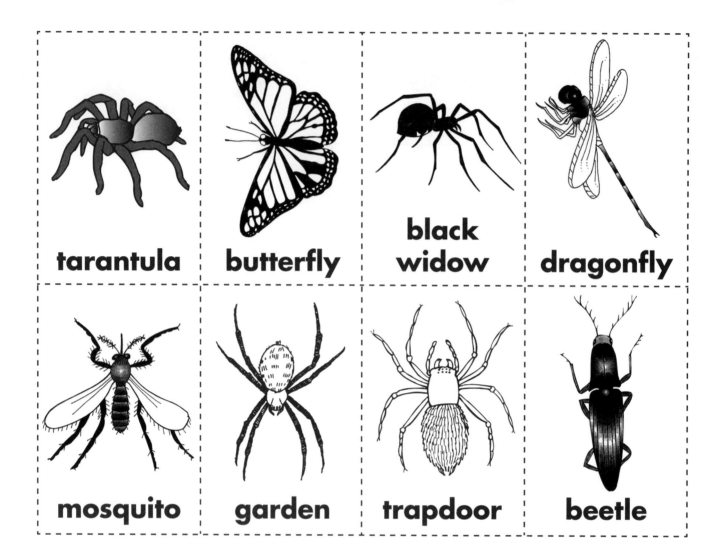

tarantula   butterfly   black widow   dragonfly

mosquito   garden   trapdoor   beetle

Science Centers—Take It to Your Seat • EMC 5002

Animal Life Cycles

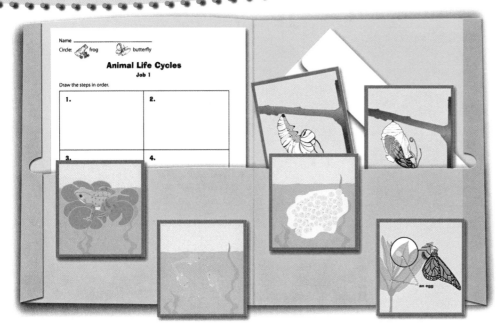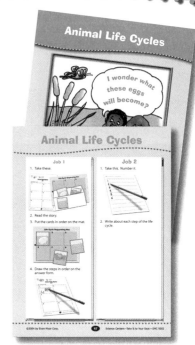

Prepare a folder following the directions on page 3. Laminate the cover design on page 45 and the student directions on page 47. Attach the cover to the front of the folder and the student directions to the back of the folder.

Preparing the Center

Job 1

1. Laminate the sequencing mat on page 49 and the sequencing cards on pages 55 and 57. Cut the cards apart. Remove the frog and butterfly life cycle booklets on pages 51 and 53. Cut around the outer edges of the page. Fold the page in half vertically. Cut on the dotted line; insert the center section into the cover section. Place each set of picture cards and its informational booklet in an envelope. Label the envelopes *Frog Life Cycle* and *Butterfly Life Cycle*.
2. Place the envelopes and the sequencing mat in the right-hand pocket of the folder.
3. Reproduce the answer form on page 44 and place copies in the left-hand pocket of the folder.

Job 2

1. Provide writing paper for students to use.
2. Place the paper in the left-hand pocket of the folder.

Using the Center

Job 1

1. The student selects one envelope and circles *frog* or *butterfly* on the answer form.
2. After reading the booklet, the student sequences the picture cards to show the animal's life cycle in order.
3. Then the student draws the stages in order on the answer form.

Job 2

1. The student numbers writing paper from 1 to 6.
2. Then the student writes about each stage of the life cycle he or she sequenced, using a word, phrase, or sentence.

Name _____

Circle:  frog   butterfly

Animal Life Cycles
Job 1

Draw the steps in order.

1.	2.
3.	4.
5.	6.

Animal Life Cycles

Animal Life Cycles

Job 1

1. Take these.

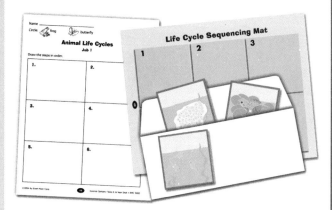

2. Read the story.

3. Put the cards in order on the mat.

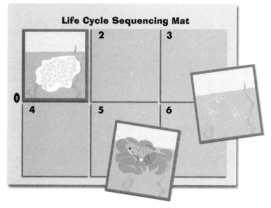

4. Draw the steps in order on the answer form.

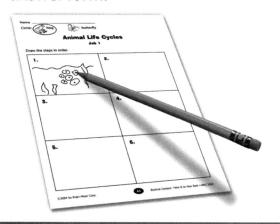

Job 2

1. Take this. Number it.

2. Write about each step of the life cycle.

Life Cycle Sequencing Mat

1

2

3

4

5

6

The tadpole grows front legs, too. It starts to eat small animals that live in the water. It looks more like a frog.

5

An egg hatches. A tadpole swims out of the egg.

2

Picture Dictionary

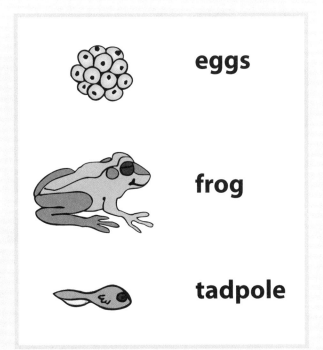

eggs

frog

tadpole

Frog

A tadpole has no legs. It breathes with gills. It swims by moving its tail. It eats tiny plants that grow in the water.

3

The tadpole grows back legs. Its tail is shorter. Now the tadpole has lungs. It swims to the top of the water to get air.

4

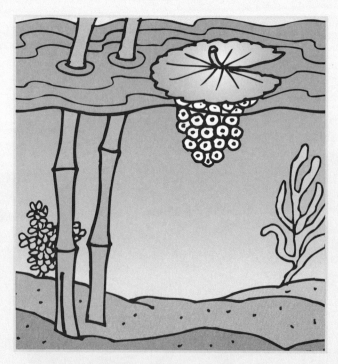

A frog lays eggs in the water. A frog egg looks like a ball of jelly with a dot inside.

1

The tadpole is a frog now. It can live on the land. It comes back to the pond to swim and to look for food.

6

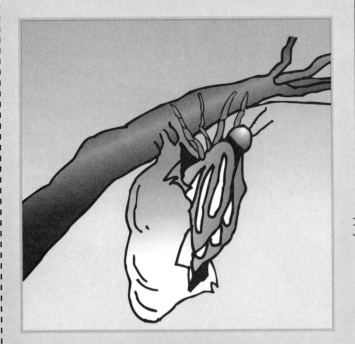

The caterpillar becomes a butterfly. The butterfly comes out of the chrysalis. Its wings are limp and wet.

5

A caterpillar hatches from the egg. It eats leaves. It grows bigger and bigger.

2

Picture Dictionary

butterfly

caterpillar

chrysalis

eggs

Butterfly

53

The caterpillar hooks itself onto a stem.

3

The caterpillar makes a cover around its body. The cover is called a chrysalis (kri' - su - lis). Inside the chrysalis, the caterpillar is changing.

4

A butterfly lays an egg on a leaf.

1

The wings dry. The butterfly flies away.

6

Frog Life Cycle Sequencing Cards

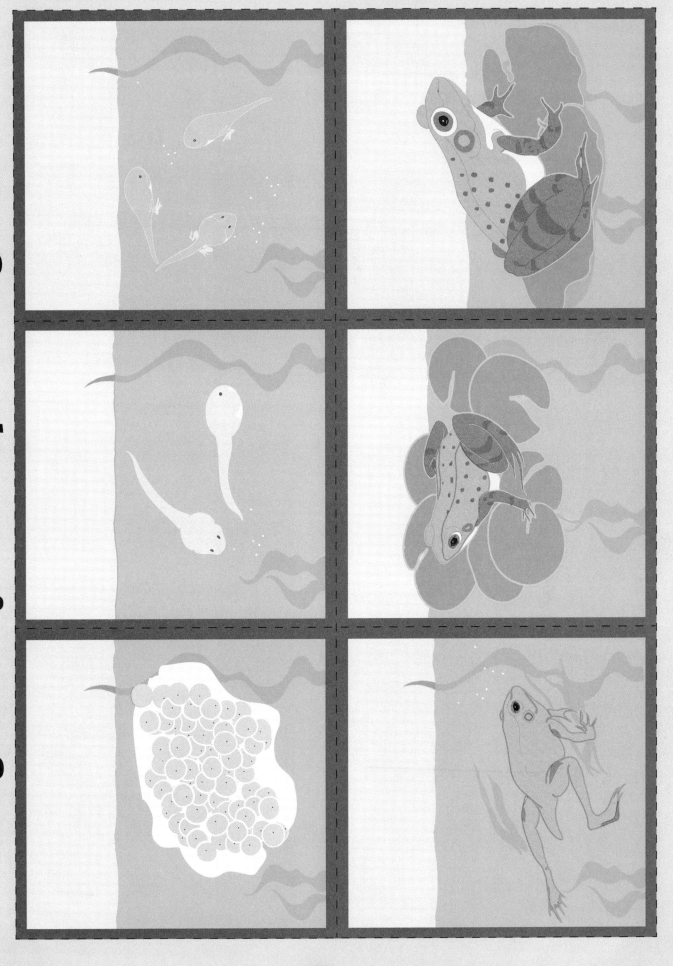

Science Centers—Take It to Your Seat • EMC 5002

Fur, Feathers, Scales

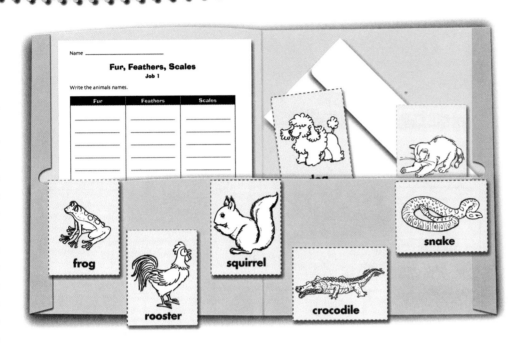
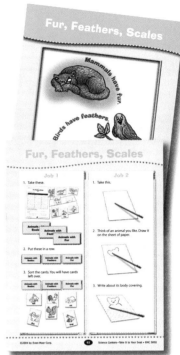

Prepare a folder following the directions on page 3. Laminate the cover design on page 61 and the student directions on page 63. Attach the cover to the front of the folder and the student directions to the back of the folder.

Preparing the Center

Job 1

1. Laminate and cut out the title cards on page 65 and the picture cards on pages 67–71. Place the picture cards in an envelope labeled *Fur, Feathers, Scales.*
2. Place the envelope and title cards in the right-hand pocket of the folder.
3. Reproduce the answer form on page 60 and place copies in the left-hand pocket of the folder.

Job 2

Place a supply of drawing paper in the left-hand pocket of the folder.

Using the Center

Job 1

1. The student places the title cards in a row, and then sorts the picture cards by placing them under the correct title. There will be three cards that do not fit any of the three categories.
2. Then the student completes the answer form by listing the animals that fit in each group and explaining why the three extras do not fit.

Job 2

1. The student draws an animal he or she likes.
2. Then the student describes its body covering.

Name _____

Fur, Feathers, Scales

Job 1

Write the animals' names in the correct column.

Fur	Feathers	Scales
_____	_____	_____
_____	_____	_____
_____	_____	_____
_____	_____	_____
_____	_____	_____
_____	_____	_____
_____	_____	_____
_____	_____	_____

Which three animals do **not** belong?

_____ _____ _____

Why not?

_____

_____

Fur, Feathers, Scales

Mammals have fur.

Birds have feathers.

Reptiles have scales.

Fur, Feathers, Scales

Job 1

1. Take these.

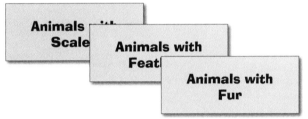

2. Put these in a row.

Animals with Scales	Animals with Feathers	Animals with Fur

3. Sort the cards. You will have cards left over.

Animals with Scales	Animals with Feathers	Animals with Fur

Job 2

1. Take this.

2. Think of an animal you like. Draw it on the sheet of paper.

3. Write about its body covering.

Animals with Scales

Animals with Feathers

Animals with Fur

©2004 by Evan-Moor Corp.

©2004 by Evan-Moor Corp.

©2004 by Evan-Moor Corp.

frog

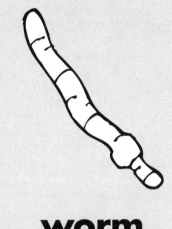

worm

octopus

dog

cat

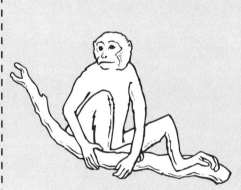

monkey

bear

kangaroo

mouse

squirrel

walrus

ostrich

penguin

rooster

robin

quail

duck

hummingbird

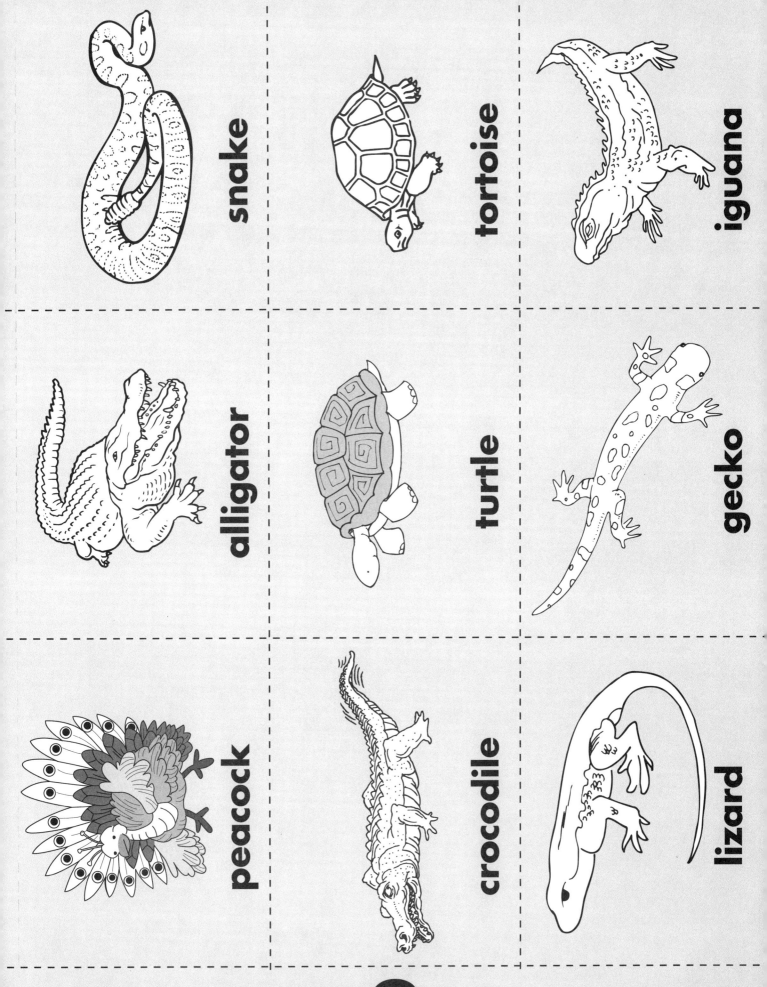

snake

tortoise

iguana

alligator

turtle

gecko

peacock

crocodile

lizard

Camouflage

Prepare a folder following the directions on page 3. Laminate the cover design on page 75 and the student directions on page 77. Attach the cover to the front of the folder and the student directions to the back of the folder.

Preparing the Center

Job 1

1. Laminate and cut out the background cards and animals on pages 79–87. Place the animals in an envelope labeled *Camouflage*.
2. Place the envelope and background cards in the right-hand pocket of the folder.
3. Reproduce the answer form on page 74 and place copies in the left-hand pocket of the folder.

Job 2

Place a supply of drawing paper in the left-hand pocket of the folder.

Using the Center

Job 1

1. The student takes the background cards and animals from the envelope.
2. The student matches each animal to the correct background. There will be three animals left over.
3. Next, the student writes the animal's name next to the card number where it was camouflaged, and then explains what helps the animals hide.

Job 2

1. The student draws a picture of an animal.
2. Then the student adds a background that will camouflage the animal.

Name _____

Camouflage
Job 1

Write the name of the animal that matches each card.

Card Number   Animal Name

1   _____

2   _____

3   _____

4   _____

5   _____

6   _____

7   _____

8   _____

9   _____

What helps these animals hide?

_____

_____

_____

          Science Centers—Take It to Your Seat • EMC 5002

Camouflage

The dark moth
can hide.

The white moth
can not hide.

Science Centers—Take It to Your Seat • EMC 5002

Camouflage

Job 1

1. Take these.

2. Match the animal to the card where it can hide.

3. Write the animal's name next to the number.

4. Tell what helps the animals hide.

Job 2

1. Take this.

2. Draw an animal.

3. Draw a background that can hide the animal.

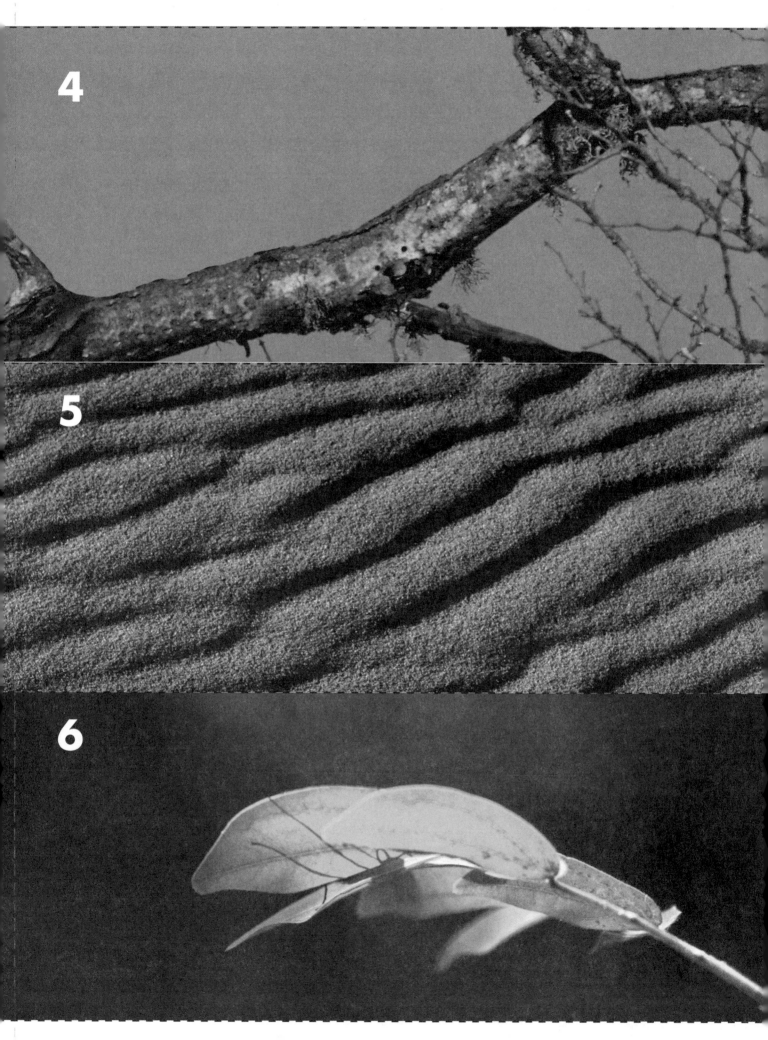

©2004 by Evan-Moor Corp.

©2004 by Evan-Moor Corp.

©2004 by Evan-Moor Corp.

arctic fox

frog

walking stick

butterfly

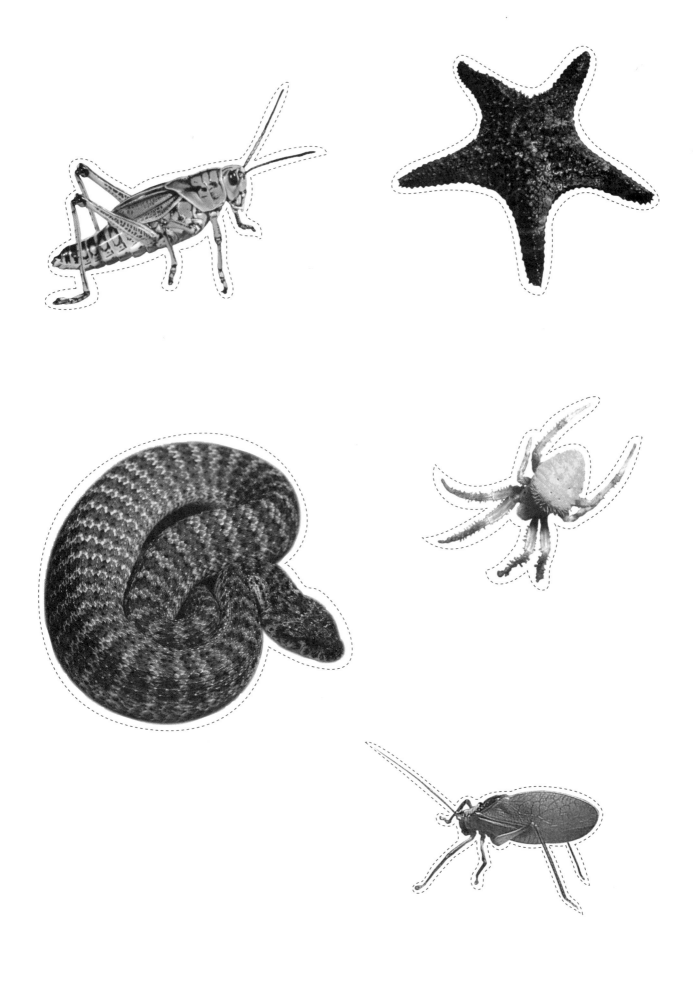

sea star

grasshopper

crab
spider

snake

katydid

88 Science Centers—Take It to Your Seat • EMC 5002

Parts of a Plant

Prepare a folder following the directions on page 3. Laminate the cover design on page 91 and the student directions on page 93. Attach the cover to the front of the folder and the student directions to the back of the folder.

Preparing the Center

Job 1
1. Laminate and cut out the puzzle pieces on pages 95 and 97. Place the pieces for each puzzle in an envelope. Label the envelopes to name the sets—*Flower* and *Tree*.
2. Place the envelopes in the right-hand pocket of the folder.
3. Reproduce the answer form on page 90 and place copies in the left-hand pocket of the folder.

Job 2
1. Reproduce the informational booklet on page 99 and the answer form on page 100.
2. Place the book and copies of the answer form in the left-hand pocket of the folder.

Using the Center

Job 1
1. The student takes the puzzle pieces from each envelope one at a time and puts them together to create a flowering plant and a tree.
2. Then the student draws each plant on the answer form and labels the parts.
3. Finally, the student compares a tree and a flowering plant.

Job 2
1. Students cut and staple the little book together.
2. The student reads the information about plant parts in the little book.
3. Then the student draws the plant parts in the correct boxes on the answer form (page 100).

Parts of a Plant
Job 1

Draw and label the parts of these plants.

Flower	**Tree**

How are a flower and a tree alike?

_____

_____

How are they different?

_____

_____

Parts of a Plant

A plant has many parts.

blossom

leaf

stem

roots

Parts of a Plant

Job 1

1. Take these.

2. Put the puzzles together.

3. Draw the plants. Name the parts.

4. Write the answers.

Job 2

1. Take these.

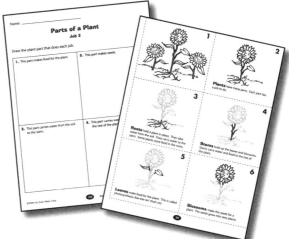

2. Make the book. Cut. Put the pages in order. Staple.

3. Draw the answers.

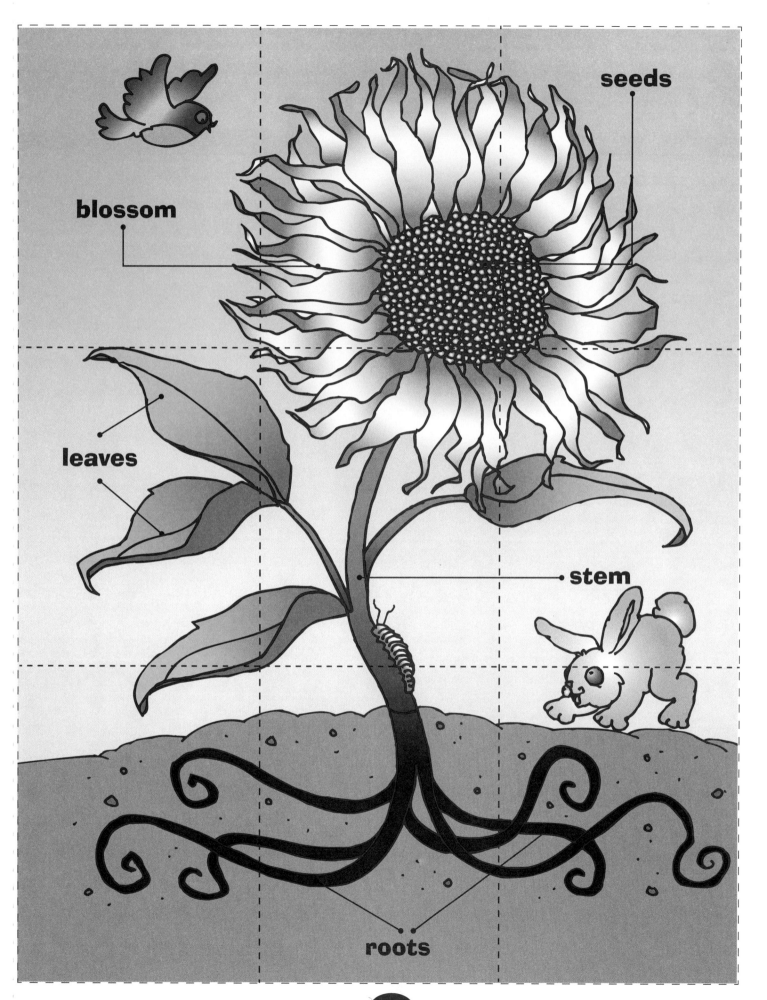

seeds

blossom

leaves

stem

roots

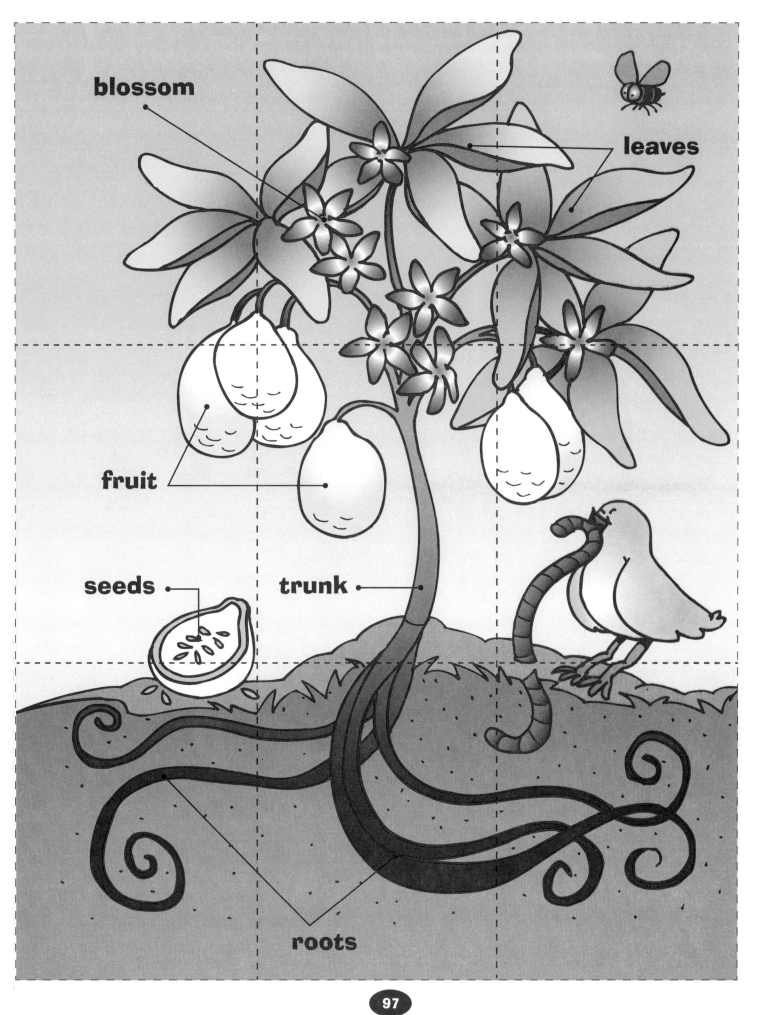

blossom

leaves

fruit

seeds

trunk

roots

1

2

Plants have many parts. Each part has a job to do.

3

Roots hold a plant in place. They take water from the soil. They carry water to the stem. Some plants store food in the roots.

4

Stems hold up the leaves and blossoms. Stems carry water and food to the rest of the plant.

5

Leaves make food for the plant. This is called photosynthesis (foe-toe-sin'-thuh-sis).

6

Blossoms make the seeds for a plant. The seeds grow into new plants.

Name _____

Parts of a Plant
Job 2

Draw the plant part that does each job.

1. This part makes food for the plant.	**2.** This part makes seeds.
3. This part carries water from the soil to the stem.	**4.** This part carries water and food to the rest of the plant.

Science Centers—Take It to Your Seat • EMC 5002

Life Cycle of a Plant

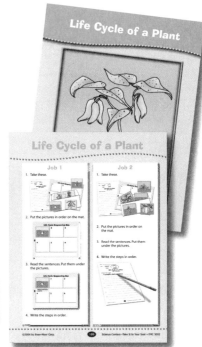

Prepare a folder following the directions on page 3. Laminate the cover design on page 103 and the student directions on page 105. Attach the cover to the front of the folder and the student directions to the back of the folder.

Preparing the Center

Job 1 and Job 2

1. Laminate the sequencing mat on page 107. Laminate and cut out the sequencing cards and sentence strips on pages 109–115.
2. Place the pumpkin cards and sentence strips in one envelope and the bean cards and sentence strips in a second envelope. Label each envelope to name the life cycle—*Pumpkin* and *Beans*.
3. Place the sequencing mat and the *Beans* envelope in the right-hand pocket of the folder. Place the *Pumpkin* envelope in the left-hand pocket.
4. Reproduce the answer form on page 102 and place copies in both pockets of the folder.

Using the Center

Job 1

1. The student takes the *Beans* envelope and places the picture cards in order on the sequencing mat.
2. Then the student reads each sentence strip and places it under the correct picture.
3. Finally, the student circles *Beans* on the answer form and writes about each stage.

Job 2

The student takes the *Pumpkin* envelope and repeats the steps, using a second copy of the same answer sheet.

Name _____

Circle:

beans   **pumpkin**

Life Cycle of a Plant
Job 1 and Job 2

Write the steps in order.

1. _____

   _____

2. _____

   _____

3. _____

   _____

4. _____

   _____

5. _____

   _____

6. _____

   _____

Life Cycle of a Plant

Bean plants grow
from bean seeds.

Science Centers—Take It to Your Seat • EMC 5002

Life Cycle of a Plant

Job 1

1. Take these.

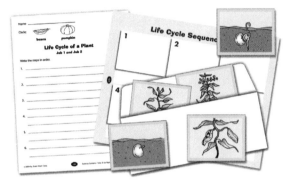

2. Put the pictures in order on the mat.

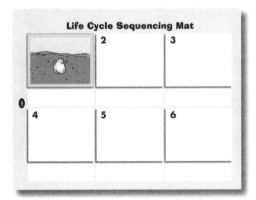

3. Read the sentences. Put them under the pictures.

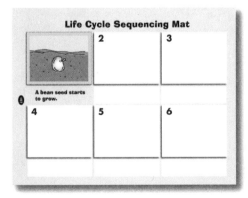

4. Write the steps in order.

Job 2

1. Take these.

2. Put the pictures in order on the mat.

3. Read the sentences. Put them under the pictures.

4. Write the steps in order.

Science Centers—Take It to Your Seat • EMC 5002

Life Cycle Sequencing Mat

1

2

3

4

5

6

Science Centers—Take It to Your Seat • EMC 5002

Bean Life Cycle Pictures

109

A bean seed starts
to grow.

Roots grow down.
A shoot grows up.

Leaves grow on
the stem.

The bean plant gets
bigger.

Blossoms grow on
the plant.

The blossoms make seeds.
The seeds grow in pods.

Science Centers—Take It to Your Seat • EMC 5002

Pumpkin Life Cycle Pictures

 Science Centers—Take It to Your Seat • EMC 5002

A pumpkin seed is planted.

Roots grow down.
A shoot grows up.

The plant grows bigger.
It has many leaves.

A blossom grows on
the plant.

Small green pumpkins
grow.

The big orange pumpkin is
ripe. It is filled with seeds.

©2004 by Evan-Moor Corp.

©2004 by Evan-Moor Corp.

©2004 by Evan-Moor Corp.

©2004 by Evan-Moor Corp.

©2004 by Evan-Moor Corp.

©2004 by Evan-Moor Corp.

We Eat Plants

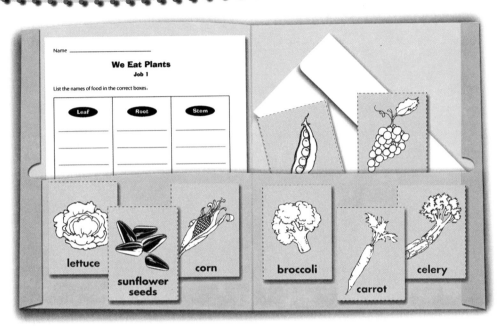

Prepare a folder following the directions on page 3. Laminate the cover design on page 119 and the student directions on page 121. Attach the cover to the front of the folder and the student directions to the back of the folder.

Preparing the Center

Job 1

1. Laminate and cut out the title cards on page 123 and the picture cards on pages 125 and 127. Place them in an envelope labeled *We Eat Plants*.
2. Place the envelope in the right-hand pocket of the folder.
3. Reproduce the answer form on page 118 and place copies in the left-hand pocket of the folder.

Job 2

Place a supply of drawing paper in the left-hand pocket of the folder.

Using the Center

Job 1

1. The student places the plant part labels in a row and sorts the picture cards according to their plant part.
2. Then the student writes the name of each vegetable or fruit under the correct heading on the answer form.

Job 2

1. The student takes a sheet of drawing paper and folds it into six boxes.
2. The student writes the name of a different plant part in each box.
3. Then the student draws his or her favorite plant food for each plant part.

Name _____

We Eat Plants

Job 1

List the names of food in the correct boxes.

Leaf	**Root**	**Stem**
_____	_____	_____
_____	_____	_____
_____	_____	_____
Flower	**Fruit**	**Seed**
_____	_____	_____
_____	_____	_____
_____	_____	_____

Science Centers—Take It to Your Seat • EMC 5002

We Eat Plants

We Eat Plants

Job 1

1. Take these.

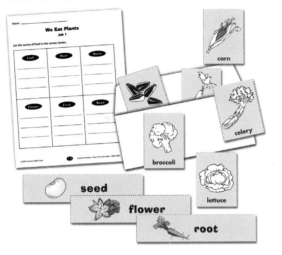

2. Put these in a row.

3. Sort the cards.

3. Write.

Job 2

1. Take this. Fold it into six boxes.

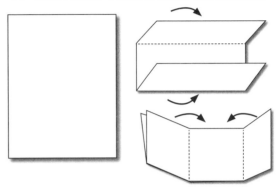

2. Write.

root	leaf
flower	seed
stem	fruit

3. Draw your favorite plant food for each part.

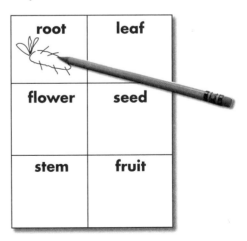

Science Centers—Take It to Your Seat • EMC 5002

 **leaf**

 **root**

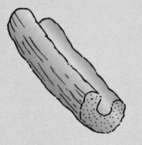 **stem**

 **flower**

 **fruit**

 **seed**

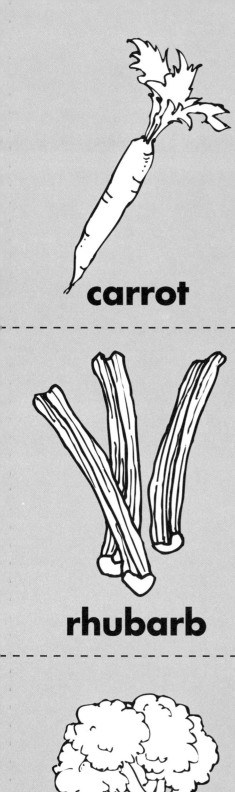 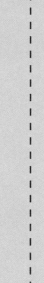

carrot

 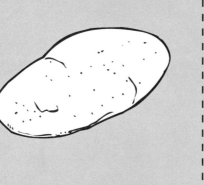

potato

radish

 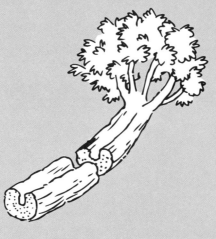

rhubarb

celery

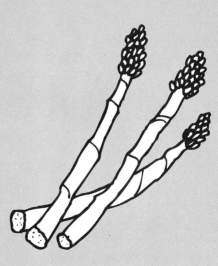

asparagus

broccoli

cauliflower

artichoke

cabbage

lettuce

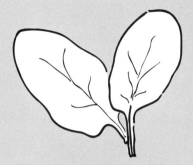

spinach

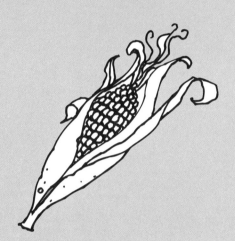

corn

sunflower seeds

peas

apple

grapes

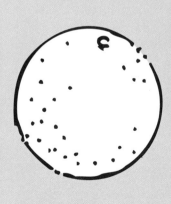

orange

Body Parts

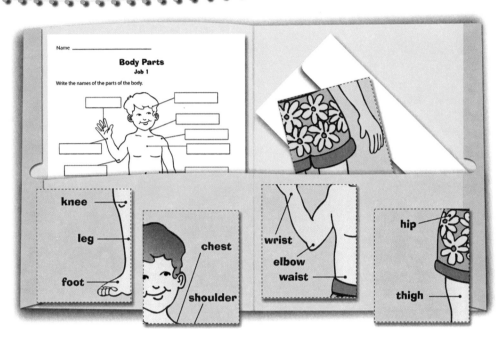

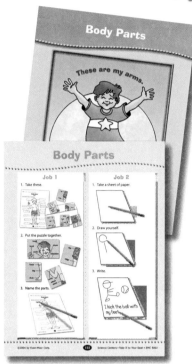

Prepare a folder following the directions on page 3. Laminate the cover design on page 131 and the student directions on page 133. Attach the cover to the front of the folder and the student directions to the back of the folder.

Preparing the Center

Job 1

1. Laminate and cut out the puzzle pieces on pages 135 and 137. Place the puzzle pieces in an envelope labeled *Body Parts*.
2. Place the envelope in the right-hand pocket of the folder.
3. Reproduce the answer form on page 130 and place copies in the left-hand pocket of the folder.

Job 2

Place a supply of drawing paper in the left-hand pocket of the folder.

Using the Center

Job 1

1. The student takes the puzzle pieces from the envelope and puts the puzzle together.
2. Using the labels on the puzzle, the student labels the body parts on the answer form.

Job 2

1. The student draws a self-portrait showing himself or herself in action.
2. Then the student describes the body parts used in the activity.

Name _____

Body Parts
Job 1

Write the names of the parts of the body.

©2004 by Evan-Moor Corp.   Science Centers—Take It to Your Seat • EMC 5002

Body Parts

These are my arms.

132

Body Parts

Job 1

1. Take these.

2. Put the puzzle together.

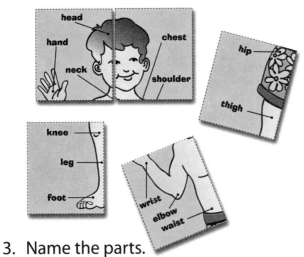

3. Name the parts.

Job 2

1. Take a sheet of paper.

2. Draw yourself.

3. Write.

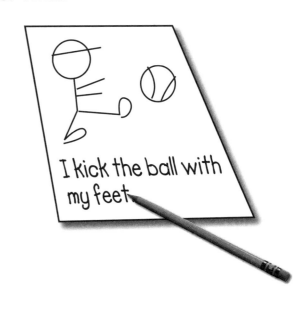

I kick the ball with my feet.

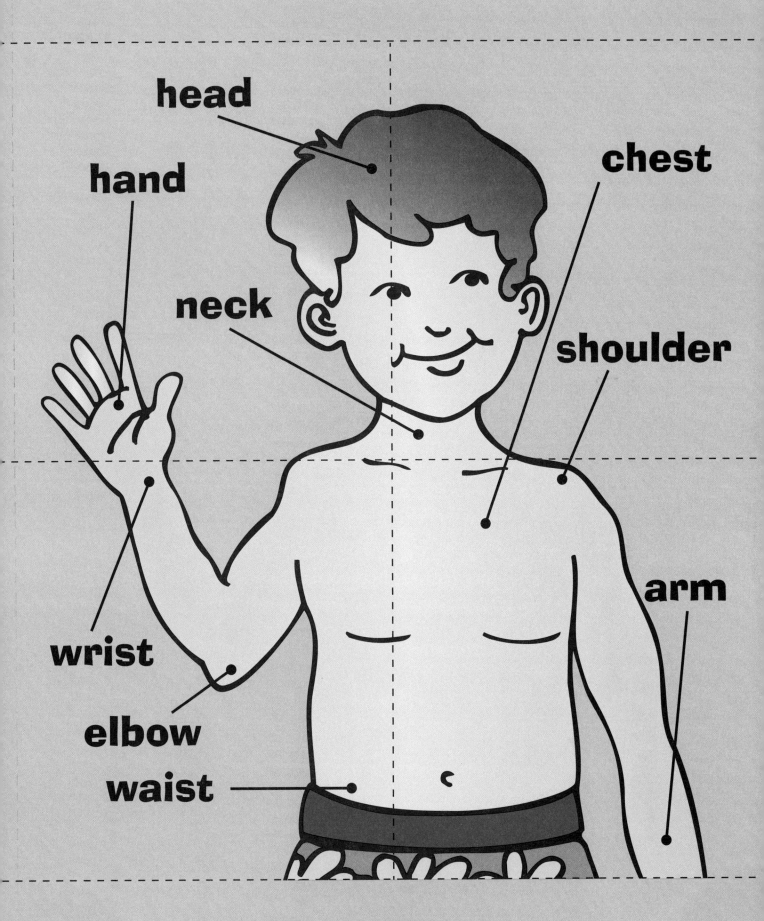

head

hand

chest

neck

shoulder

wrist

arm

elbow

waist

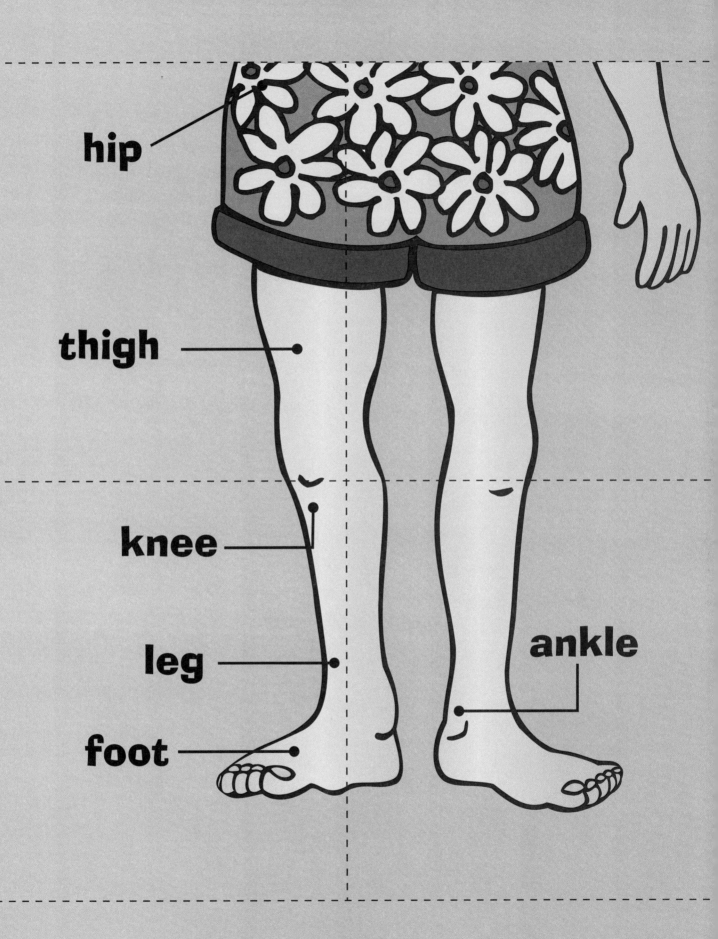

hip

thigh

knee

leg

ankle

foot

Sun, Earth, and Moon

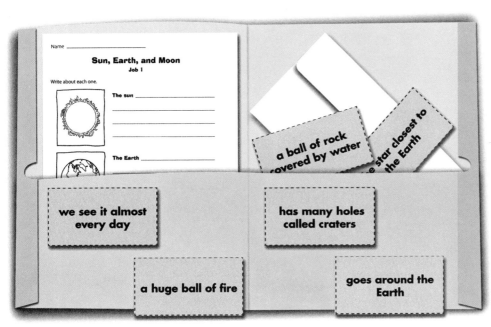

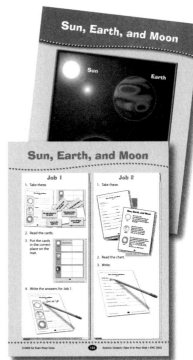

Prepare a folder following the directions on page 3. Laminate the cover design on page 141 and the student directions on page 143. Attach the cover to the front of the folder and the student directions to the back of the folder.

Preparing the Center

Job 1

1. Laminate the sorting mat on page 145 and the cards on page 147. Cut the cards apart and place them in an envelope labeled *Sun, Earth, and Moon.*
2. Place the envelope and the sorting mat in the right-hand pocket of the folder.
3. Reproduce the answer form on page 140 and place copies in the left-hand pocket of the folder.

Job 2

1. Reproduce the chart on page 149 and the answer form on page 150.
2. Place the chart and copies of the answer form in the left-hand pocket of the folder.

Using the Center

Job 1

1. The student reads the cards and places them on the sorting mat.
2. Then the student writes a paragraph about the sun, the earth, and the moon on the answer form.

Job 2

1. The student reads the chart.
2. Then the student answers questions on the answer form (page 150).

Name _____

Sun, Earth, and Moon
Job 1

Write about each one.

The sun _____

_____

_____

_____

The Earth _____

_____

_____

_____

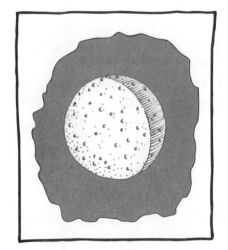

The moon _____

_____

_____

_____

Science Centers—Take It to Your Seat • EMC 5002

Sun, Earth, and Moon

Sun

Earth

Moon

Sun, Earth, and Moon

Job 1

1. Take these.

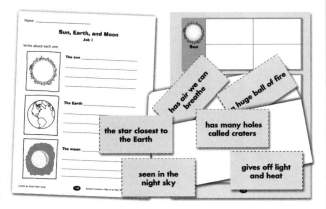

2. Read the cards.

3. Put the cards in the correct place on the mat.

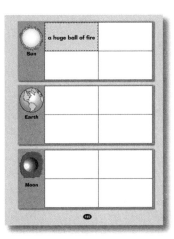

4. Write the answers for Job 1.

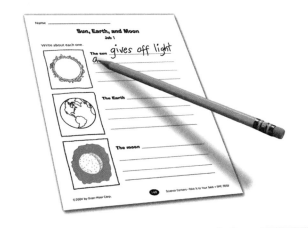

Job 2

1. Take these.

2. Read the chart.

3. Write.

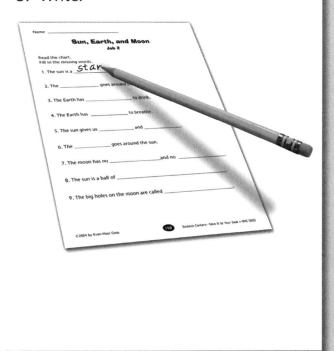

Sun, Earth, and Moon

Science Centers—Take It to Your Seat • EMC 5002

144

Sun

Earth

Moon

a huge ball of fire	the star closest to the Earth
we see it almost every day	gives off light and heat
goes around the Earth	seen in the night sky
seems to change shape	has many holes called craters
a planet	moves around the sun
a ball of rock covered by water	has air we can breathe

Sun, Earth, and Moon

Sun

The sun is a star.

It is a big ball of burning gas.

We see it almost every day.

The sun gives heat and light to the Earth.

Earth

The Earth is a planet.

It goes around the sun.

The Earth is a ball of rock.

It has water we can drink.

It has air we can breathe.

Moon

The moon goes around the Earth.

It is smaller than the Earth and sun.

There is no air on the moon.

There is no water on the moon.

There are many big holes on the moon.

The holes are called craters.

Name _____

Sun, Earth, and Moon
Job 2

Read the chart.
Fill in the missing words.

1. The sun is a _____.

2. The _____ goes around the Earth.

3. The Earth has _____ to drink.

4. The Earth has _____ to breathe.

5. The sun gives us _____ and _____.

6. The _____ goes around the sun.

7. The moon has no _____ and no _____.

8. The sun is a ball of _____.

9. The big holes on the moon are called _____.

Energy

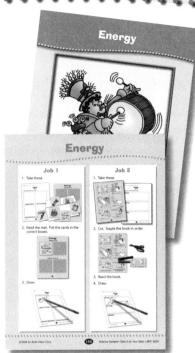

Prepare a folder following the directions on page 3. Laminate the cover design on page 153 and the student directions on page 155. Attach the cover to the front of the folder and the student directions to the back of the folder.

Preparing the Center

Job 1

1. Tape pages 157 and 159 together and then laminate them to form a sorting mat. Fold the mat in half and place it in the right-hand side of the folder.
2. Laminate and cut apart the cards on pages 161 and 163. Place the cards in an envelope labeled *Energy*. Place the envelope in the right-hand pocket of the folder.
3. Reproduce the answer form on page 152 and place copies in the left-hand pocket of the folder.

Job 2

1. Reproduce the information booklet on page 165 and the answer form on page 166.
2. Place the copies in the left-hand pocket of the folder.

Using the Center

Job 1

1. Students take the cards from the envelope and place them in the correct boxes on the sorting mat.
2. Then students think of one more item that could go in each box and draw it on the answer form.

Job 2

1. Students cut and staple the little book together.
2. After reading the little book, students draw pictures to complete the answer form (page 166).

Name _____

Energy
Job 1

Draw something else that can go in each box.

Energy makes things move.	**Energy makes things warm up.**
Energy makes things make noise.	**Energy makes things make light.**

Energy

Energy

Job 1

1. Take these.

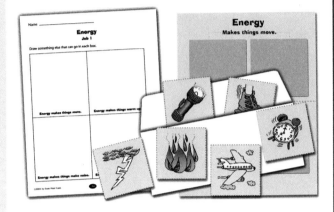

2. Read the mat. Put the cards in the correct boxes.

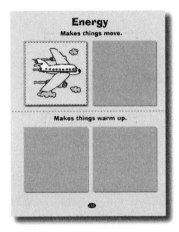

3. Draw.

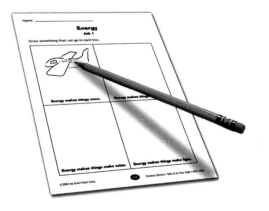

Job 2

1. Take these.

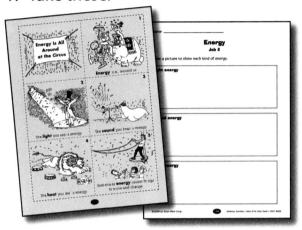

2. Cut. Staple the book in order.

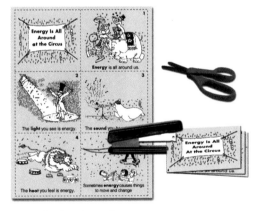

3. Read the book.

4. Draw.

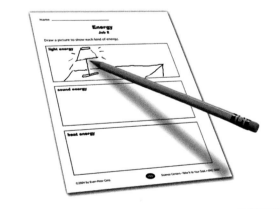

Energy

Makes things move.

Makes things warm up.

You can't see energy,
but you can see what it does.
Makes things make noise.

Makes things make light.

All because of energy.

Energy Is All Around At the Circus

1

Energy is all around us.

2

The **light** you see is energy.

3

The **sound** you hear is energy.

4

The **heat** you feel is energy.

5

Sometimes **energy** causes things to move and change.

Name _____

Energy

Job 2

Draw a picture to show each kind of energy.

light energy

sound energy

heat energy

Weather

Prepare a folder following the directions on page 3. Laminate the cover design on page 169 and the student directions on page 171. Attach the cover to the front of the folder and the student directions to the back of the folder.

Preparing the Center

Job 1
1. Laminate and cut out the cards on pages 173 and 175. Place the cards in an envelope labeled *Weather*. (Be sure to mix them up!)
2. Place the envelope in the right-hand pocket of the folder.
3. Reproduce the answer form on page 168 and place copies in the left-hand pocket of the folder.

Job 2
1. Reproduce the answer forms on pages 177 and 178.
2. Place copies in the left-hand pocket of the folder.

Using the Center

Job 1
1. Students take the envelope and look at each card.
2. They determine if the card shows something related to hot weather or cold weather, and then circle the card number on the answer form, using the appropriate color for hot and for cold.
3. Then students describe the current weather.

Job 2
1. On the answer form (page 177), students list what they like to do in each type of weather.
2. On the second answer form (page 178), students draw themselves dressed for an activity they like to do in each type of weather.

Name _____

Weather

Job 1

Take two crayons. Circle the card numbers.

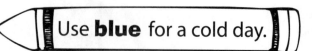

Use **red** for a hot day.   Use **blue** for a cold day.

| 1 | 2 | 3 | 4 | 5 | 6 | 7 | 8 |

| 9 | 10 | 11 | 12 | 13 | 14 | 15 | 16 |

| 17 | 18 | 19 | 20 | 21 | 22 | 23 | 24 |

Tell what your weather is like today.

_____

_____

_____

Weather

Job 1

1. Take these.

2. Look at a card.

3. Circle its number.

   red = a hot day   blue = a cold day

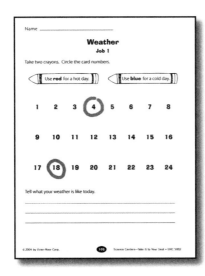

4. Answer the question.

Job 2

1. Take these.

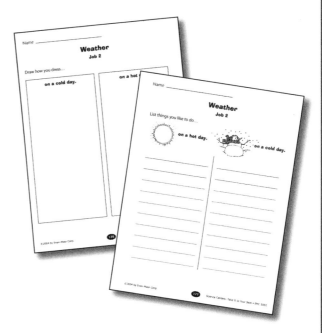

2. List things you like to do.

3. Draw what you like to do.

1

3

4

8

10

11

15

16

17

20

22

23

Weather

Job 2

List things you like to do…

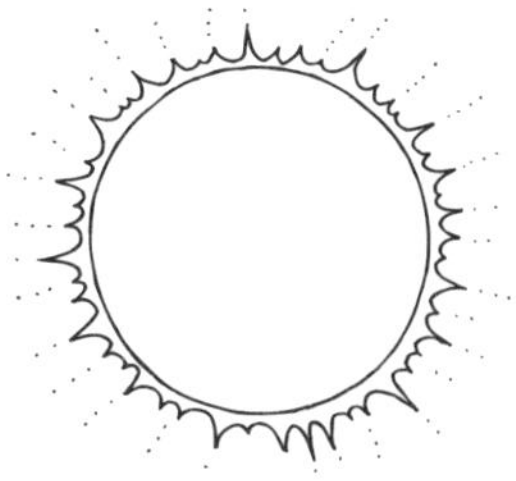

on a hot day.

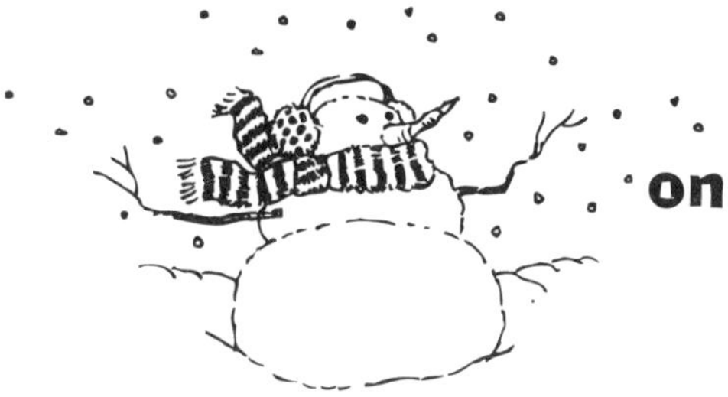

on a cold day.

_____

_____

_____

_____

_____

_____

_____

_____

_____

_____

_____

_____

_____

_____

Name _____

Weather

Job 2

Draw how you dress…

on a cold day.	on a hot day.

More Work or Less Work?

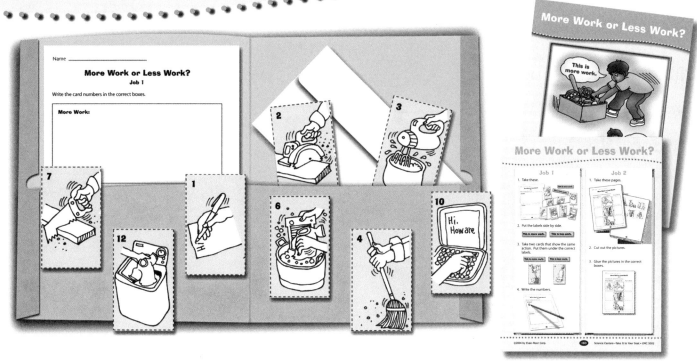

Prepare a folder following the directions on page 3. Laminate the cover design on page 181 and the student directions on page 183. Attach the cover to the front of the folder and the student directions to the back of the folder.

Preparing the Center

Job 1

1. Laminate and cut apart the labels and picture cards on page 185. Place them in an envelope labeled *More Work or Less Work?*
2. Place the envelope in the right-hand pocket of the folder.
3. Reproduce the answer form on page 180 and place copies in the left-hand pocket of the folder.

Job 2

1. Reproduce the answer form on page 187 and the pictures on page 188.
2. Place copies in the left-hand pocket of the folder.

Using the Center

Job 1

1. Students take the labels and cards from the envelope.
2. They place the labels side by side and sort the cards under the headings.
3. Then students write the numbers of the cards in the correct boxes on the answer form.

Job 2

1. Students take the answer form (page 187) and a page of pictures to cut out.
2. After cutting out the pictures, students glue the pictures in the correct boxes on the answer form.

More Work or Less Work?

Job 1

Write the card numbers in the correct boxes.

More Work:

Less Work:

More Work or Less Work?

More Work or Less Work?

Job 1

1. Take these.

2. Put the labels side by side.

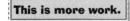

3. Take two cards that show the same action. Put them under the correct labels.

4. Write the numbers.

Job 2

1. Take these pages.

2. Cut out the pictures.

3. Glue the pictures in the correct boxes.

This is more work. | This is less work.

1

10

Hi.
How are

4

8

2

7

5

9

3

11

6

12

Name _____

More Work or Less Work?
Job 2

Cut out the pictures. Glue them in the correct boxes.

This job is **more** work.   This job takes work.   This job is **less** work.

Answer Key

Page 4 – Living or Not Living?

Job 1 – Set 1

Living	Not Living
turtle	rock
tree	shoe
monkey	book
bird	box
dog	car
flower	flag

Job 1 – Set 2

Living	Not Living
butterfly	chair
fish	basket
beetle	bike
girl	cookie
duck	computer
pony	teddy bear

Job 2

These should be colored:
boy, bird, dog, tree, bug, plant

Written answers will vary, but must include three of these:
    They eat.
    They grow.
    They move.
    They reproduce.

Page 17 – What Goes Together?

Job 1

Answers will vary, but must reflect the task. For example: the flamingo, the hawk, the parrot, and the penguin—They all have feathers.

Job 2

Answers will vary, but must reflect the task. For example: the zebra, the dog, and the lizard—They all have 4 legs.

Page 31 – Spiders and Insects

Job 1

Only spiders have:
    8 legs
    2 body parts
    spinnerets
    most have 8 eyes
    palps

Only insects have:
    6 legs
    3 body parts
    2 eyes
    antennae
    most have wings

Both have:
    a hard outer skin
    a mouth

Job 2

Spiders: tarantula, black widow, garden, trapdoor

Insects: butterfly, dragonfly, mosquito, beetle

Written answers will vary, but must contain some characteristics of a spider and of an insect.

Page 43 – Animal Life Cycles
Job 1

Students should draw steps for one of the following life cycles:

life cycle of frog

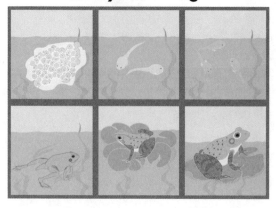

life cycle of butterfly

Job 2

Students should write about the stages of the life cycle of a frog or butterfly. The wording will vary, but must contain a word, phrase, or sentence about each stage.

Page 59 – Fur, Feathers, Scales

Job 1

Fur	Feathers	Scales
dog	ostrich	alligator
cat	penguin	snake
monkey	rooster	crocodile
bear	robin	turtle
kangaroo	quail	tortoise
mouse	duck	lizard
squirrel	hummingbird	gecko
walrus	peacock	iguana

These three do <u>not</u> belong:
worm, frog, octopus
They do not have fur or feathers or scales.
OR They all have smooth skin.

Job 2

Drawings and written work will vary, but must show an animal and describe its outside covering.

Page 73 – Camouflage
Job 1

1. crab spider
2. arctic fox
3. frog
4. walking stick
5. snake
6. katydid
7. grasshopper
8. sea star
9. butterfly

Their colors do not show on the cards.

Job 2

Drawings will vary, but must illustrate camouflage.

Page 89 – Parts of a Plant
Job 1

Drawings will vary, but must show a flowering plant and a tree with these parts labeled—
flowering plant: roots, stem, leaves, blossom, seeds
tree: roots, leaves, trunk, blossom, fruit, seeds

Answers will vary, but must be accurate.
For example: Alike – They both have leaves.
Different – A tree stem is thicker than a flower stem.

Job 2
Drawings of:
1. a leaf   3. roots
2. a blossom   4. a stem

Page 101– Life Cycle of a Plant
Job 1
The steps may be written in the student's own words, but must be in this order:

1. A bean seed starts to grow.
2. Roots grow down.
   A shoot grows up.
3. Leaves grow on the stem.
4. The bean plant gets bigger.
5. Blossoms grow on the plant.
6. The blossoms make seeds.
   The seeds grow in pods.

Job 2
The steps may be written in the student's own words, but must be in this order:

1. A pumpkin seed is planted.
2. Roots grow down.
   A shoot grows up.
3. The plant grows bigger.
   It has many leaves.
4. A blossom grows on the plant.
5. Small green pumpkins grow.
6. The big orange pumpkin is ripe.
   It is filled with seeds.

Page 117 – We Eat Plants
Job 1

Leaf
1. cabbage
2. lettuce
3. spinach

Root
1. carrot
2. potato
3. radish

Stem
1. rhubarb
2. celery
3. asparagus

Flower
1. broccoli
2. cauliflower
3. artichoke

Fruit
1. apple
2. orange
3. grapes

Seed
1. corn
2. beans
3. peas

Job 2
Drawings will vary, but should reflect the correct plant part.

Page 129 – Body Parts
Job 1

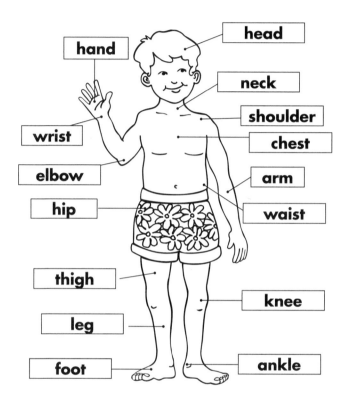

Job 2
Drawings and written work will vary, but should show and describe parts of the body in action.

Page 139 – Sun, Earth, and Moon
Job 1
Answers will vary, but could include answers such as:

The sun is a ball of fire.
The sun is a star.
The sun gives off heat and light.
The Earth goes around the sun.
The Earth has air we can breathe.
The Earth is a planet.
The moon is seen in the night sky.
The moon seems to change shape.
The moon has many holes called craters.

Job 2

1. star
2. moon
3. water
4. air
5. heat; light
6. Earth
7. water; air
8. burning gas
9. craters

Page 151 – Energy

Job 1

Drawings will vary, but could include:

Energy makes things move: roller blade, airplane.

Energy makes things warm up: soup, campfire.

Energy makes things make noise: alarm clock, horn.

Energy makes things make light: flashlight, lightning.

Job 2

Drawings will vary, but must show these kinds of energy: heat, light, and sound.

Page 167 – Weather

Job 1

Circled in **red:** 2, 5, 6, 7, 9, 12, 13, 14, 18, 19, 21, 24

Circled in **blue:** 1, 3, 4, 8, 10, 11, 15, 16, 17, 20, 22, 23

Written answers will vary.

Job 2

Part 1 - Lists will vary.
Part 2 - Drawings will vary.

Page 179 – More Work or Less Work?

Job 1

More work: 1, 4, 6, 7, 9, 11
Less work: 2, 3, 5, 8, 10, 12

Job 2